Garmin Forerunner 165 & 965 Fitness Watch User Guide

A Manual for Garmin Smartwatch Setup, GPS, Tips, Tricks, Troubleshooting, and Fitness Tracking for Beginners and Seniors

Justin C. Rosson

Copyright

Table of content

Introduction

This book serves as a comprehensive guide for users of the Garmin Forerunner 165 & 965 smartwatches. It will go beyond technical instructions to include real-life stories from users who have harnessed the power of these devices to enhance their fitness journeys. The book will not only detail the functionality of the smartwatches but will also inspire readers by showcasing diverse experiences and transformations through Garmin technology.

Chapter 1
Getting Your Garmin Forerunner Started

Unpacking and Preliminary Configuration

Opening the package on your new Garmin Forerunner 165 or 965 is like embarking on a brand-new fitness and health tracking journey. It's the first step to a world of opportunities that can track your health, improve your exercises, and inspire you. Let's discuss the key components that will enable you to get started smoothly as we embark on this wonderful voyage.

Summary of the Items Included

When you carefully open the package, you're met with a meticulously curated collection of accessories made to go well with your new smartwatch. Inside, you will discover:

• **The main attraction is the Garmin Forerunner Watch!** This device is designed for performance and is both lightweight and durable.

• **Charging Cable:** Say goodbye to fumbling with random cords! Easily snapping into position, this magnetic charging cable guarantees a reliable connection each and every time.

• **Quick Start Manual:** Although you may be tempted to ignore it, this manual contains important information that will guide you through using your new device.

• **Safety Information:** Crucial instructions to maintain the best possible condition for both you and your watch.

Spend a moment getting acquainted with these things. For your Garmin experience to be as seamless as possible, each part is essential.

Procedure for Device Charging

You have to charge your Garmin before you can start using its many capabilities. Here's how:

1. Connect the Charging Cable: Attach the charging cable's USB end to your computer or a power adapter. Make sure the connection is secure.

2. Align the Connectors: Place the cable's other end close to the watch's rear. The magnetic connectors will snap into position, as you can see. It resembles magic!

3. Charging Status: A charging icon will appear on your watch after it has been connected. Until it is fully charged, which normally takes two hours, keep it plugged in. Depending on usage, a full charge will last your watch for many days.

You can think about your fitness objectives while your watch charges. Are you trying to stay active, track your heart health, or increase your running time? You may improve your experience from the beginning by establishing clear intentions.

Installing the Garmin Connect App and Configuring It

You must download the Garmin Connect app in order to fully utilize your Forerunner's capabilities. This app serves as your fitness journey's command center. To begin, follow these steps:

1. Download the app: Open the app store on your device, such as the App Store for iOS or Google Play for Android. Look up "Garmin Connect" and select "download." It's simple to use and free!

2. Create Your Account: Launch the app after downloading it. If you do not already have an account, you will need to create one. Enter your information, including your health indicators and fitness objectives. The app can customize insights for you thanks to this customization.

3. Pair Your Watch: To pair your Garmin Forerunner, follow the instructions in the app. Make sure your phone has Bluetooth turned on. Just choose your watch when it pops up in the app and make sure the pairing code is the same on both devices.

4. Adjust Settings: look around the app! Change the notification settings, select your desired unit of measurement (metric or imperial), and explore the features. Here, you may customize your Garmin experience to fit your fitness requirements and lifestyle.

5. Examine Features: Spend some time getting acquainted with the user interface of the software. The Garmin Connect app is your key to staying involved in your health journey, whether you're setting up activity tracking, looking through the health data dashboard, or finding community features.

By taking these first steps, you're starting a journey toward better health and fitness rather than merely opening a watch. The Garmin Forerunner is made to be your partner, supporting, encouraging, and acknowledging your progress as you go. Your adventure starts here, and the possibilities are endless, regardless of your level of experience as an athlete or your age as a senior trying to keep an eye on your health. Get excited, then! Awaiting you is your Garmin journey!

Creating Your Garmin Account in Parts One and Two

To get the most out of your Forerunner 165 or 965 fitness watch, you must first create a Garmin account. This straightforward but essential procedure links your smartwatch to the Garmin ecosystem, giving you access to a multitude of functions catered to your fitness journey, such as the ability to log your activities and evaluate your health metrics. Let's dissect it in detail.

How to Create an Account on Garmin

To begin, go to the Garmin Connect app, which serves as your entry point for controlling all of the information that your watch gathers. You may locate it in the Google Play Store or App Store if you haven't installed it yet. Open the app after downloading it, then choose "Create Account." A password, email address, and name are among the essential details you'll need to supply.

Remember to choose a strong password that is easy to remember but difficult to guess. It is ideal to use a mix of special characters, numbers, and letters. Read the privacy statement and terms of service after completing the needed fields. Tap "Create Account" after agreeing to them (they're worth looking at, especially if you're worried about data privacy).

You will receive a verification email after your account is created. In order to validate your account, click the link in that email. To keep your account safe and accessible only to you, this step is crucial. You are now formally a member of the Garmin family!

Connecting the app to your smartwatch

Now that you have created your Garmin account, it's time to link your Forerunner to the app. Verify that your watch is turned on and charged. You will be prompted to add a new device when you launch the

Garmin Connect app. From the list, pick your Forerunner model.

You will be guided through the matching process by the app. Usually, this is just turning on Bluetooth on your phone and choosing your watch from a list of compatible gadgets. A pairing code will show up on both your phone and watch once you tap on your watch. Verify that the codes match, and your watch will be instantly connected to your Garmin account!

What makes this relationship so crucial, then? Your fitness data may be seamlessly synced by connecting your smartwatch to the app. The data is immediately posted to your Garmin account each time you finish an activity, be it a vigorous exercise, a leisurely jog, or a brisk walk. This makes it simpler to set and meet exercise goals by enabling you to track your performance over time.

Configuring notifications and privacy preferences

After connecting your watch, it's time to personalize your experience by configuring privacy and notification settings. Navigate to the settings menu of the app. You may select the alerts you would like to receive on your watch here. You may customize your notifications to make sure you only get the most pertinent information, whether they be calls, texts, or app alerts. Receiving updates on your workout objectives or reminders to be active can be tremendously motivating for fitness aficionados. Seniors who want to minimize distractions from notifications may nevertheless want to receive important alerts about calls and messages.

Taking control of your privacy settings is equally vital. Although Garmin values user privacy, you have the ability to decide what data is shared and with whom. You can choose within the app whether to make your activity data public or private. Sharing private health information should be done with caution, particularly for elderly people who are keeping an eye on particular medical concerns. You can have a customized experience that inspires you without being overpowering by controlling these choices. Keep in mind that this is your path. Make it fit your way of life!

Setting up your Garmin account and connecting your smartwatch prepares you for a life-changing workout. Now that your account is set up, you can take advantage of every feature that your Forerunner 165 or 965 has to offer. This stage gives you the resources you need to properly track your health and connects you to a community of fitness enthusiasts in addition to your watch. So, seize the chance to explore, personalize, and enjoy the voyage that lies ahead!

Chapter 2

Understanding the features of fitness tracking

Comprehending Fitness Metrics

Understanding the stats that your Garmin Forerunner 165 or 965 offers can change your life in the data-rich realm of fitness tracking. These indicators provide a personal dashboard for seniors interested in health monitoring and fitness aficionados, allowing them to measure their progress, set objectives, and make well-informed health decisions. Now let's explore the three main indicators you will see: heart rate, steps, and calories burned. Fitness watch users must understand these factors to maximize their watch.

Heart Rate: A Signal from Your Body

One of the most important measures of your general level of fitness is your heart rate. It is a clear indication of how effectively your body is working when you are exercising. Your heart rate is continuously monitored by the Garmin Forerunner, which provides information on the resting, moderate, aerobic, anaerobic, and maximum heart rate zones.

1. Resting Heart Rate: Usually taken first thing in the morning, this is your heart rate at total rest. Better cardiovascular fitness is typically indicated by a lower resting heart rate for fitness aficionados. Using this measure, seniors can keep an eye on their heart health and spot any unexpected increases that can call for a checkup.

2. Goal Heart Rate Zones: You may maximize your workouts by being aware of your goal heart rate zone. For example, strive for the aerobic zone, where your heart rate is high but manageable, if your objective is to increase endurance. Keep your exercises productive and effective by using the Garmin's customized alerts to let you know when you approach or leave your target zone.

Example from the Real World: Let's say you are preparing for a 10K run. You can find out that running at a specific pace places you in the anaerobic zone by monitoring your heart rate. With this knowledge, you can modify your training plan and even add extra interval training to increase your speed without going overboard.

Step Count: Not Just a Count

With good reason, step tracking is a common feature in fitness watches. For many users, it provides a measurable objective and promotes movement throughout the day. Every step you take is tracked by the Garmin Forerunner, which gives you information about how active you are.

1. Daily Goals: A daily step target, usually 10,000 steps, can serve as a source of motivation. What if you're a senior who wants to continue being active? As your fitness level increases, progressively raise your initial, reasonable objective depending on your current exercise level.

2. Recognizing Activity Levels: The watch helps you determine when you might need to get up and move by dividing your daily steps into active and sedentary phases. Seniors who might have to spend a lot of time sitting down will find this extremely helpful.

An example from the real world might be a busy professional who is constantly glued to their desk. They can use the Forerunner to establish hourly reminders to move. They observe a rise in their step count and, more significantly, an increase in their energy levels following a week of tracking.

Calories Burned: Providing Energy for Your Fitness Adventure

Monitoring your caloric consumption is essential to comprehending how much energy your activities require. Based on the kind, duration, and heart rate of your activity, your Garmin watch calculates how many calories you burn.

1. Being Aware of Your Basal Metabolic Rate (BMR): Your BMR is the number of calories your body requires to sustain essential physiological processes. Knowing this figure can help you adjust your calorie intake to achieve your fitness objectives, whether they are muscle growth, weight loss, or maintenance.

2. Calories Burned During Action vs. Resting: The Garmin Forerunner makes a distinction between calories burned during action and rest. This makes it simpler to modify your diet or exercise regimen since you can observe how your workouts affect your total energy expenditure.

Real-World Example: Let's say you're trying to lose weight. You can make better choices by tracking your workout calories and comparing them to your diet. Even while running burns a lot of calories, you may have noticed that your post-workout snacks need some improvement.

The Value of Monitoring for Individual Fitness Objectives

Every one of these measurements has a distinct function in your quest for fitness. They give exercise fanatics measurable information to push boundaries and set personal records. Seniors can better manage illnesses like heart disease or hypertension by using these measurements to stay proactive about their health.

Monitoring your development gives you the ability to make wise choices. Understanding your body and its requirements is more important than simply knowing the numbers. Gaining knowledge from your Garmin can result in more pleasurable exercises, increased motivation, and eventually a healthier way of living. Please remember that your fitness journey is unique as you learn these measures. Enjoy the process of becoming a better version of yourself, acknowledge minor accomplishments, and modify your objectives as necessary.

Tailoring Your Exercise Objectives

Establishing and tailoring your exercise objectives is similar to creating a unique road map for your health path. Making a meaningful journey that reflects your goals and way of life is more important than simply reaching a goal distance or a number on a scale. You can customize your fitness path to meet your specific demands with the Garmin Forerunner 165 and 965.

How to Use the App to Set Personal Fitness Goals

Let's start by exploring the Garmin Connect app. For all things Garmin, here is your command center. The app's user-friendly layout makes goal setting seem less intimidating when you first launch it. Navigate to the "Goals" section first. Here, you can select a variety of goals, such as reaching a particular number of steps, jogging a certain distance, or even concentrating on the amount of time you spend working out each week.

1. **Select Your Goal Type:** Consider what you find meaningful. Do you want to increase your daily step count, run a 5K, or maybe set a weekly goal for active time? Choosing the appropriate objective is essential. For instance, a step target could be more appropriate

than an intense running objective if you're a senior trying to improve your mobility.

2. Establish Your Target: After deciding on a target type, it's time to establish the details. Try to push yourself while remaining realistic! For a few weeks, try to get 5,000 steps per day if you presently walk 4,000, then progressively raise it. Keep in mind that the Garmin ecosystem adapts to your pace, which is its greatest feature.

3. Establish a Deadline: Setting a deadline for yourself increases accountability. Perhaps your goal is to be accomplished in three months or by the conclusion of a particular event, such as a fitness challenge or family get-together. This helps you stay inspired and on course.

4. Save and Track: Press save to see your objectives appear in the app. During workouts, the Forerunner will remind you of your goals, which can be a useful incentive when you're having trouble tying your shoes.

Monitoring Development and Modifying Objectives Over Time

Reaching your objectives is more like a twisting road with sporadic deviations than a straight line. Maintaining motivation requires routinely reviewing your progress. The Garmin Connect app makes it simple to see how far you've come by giving you a visual depiction of your accomplishments.

1. Examine frequently: Every week, set aside time to assess your progress. How many steps did you take last week, according to the statistics? Have you met your fitness goals? This involves reviewing your work and dedication, not just the numbers.

2. Modify as Necessary: You should step up the challenge if you find yourself routinely exceeding your objectives. It's completely acceptable to readjust if you've been having difficulties. Consider taking 8,000 steps for a period rather than 10,000. Being adaptable is essential; the goal is to establish a pattern that lasts rather than burn out.

3. Mark Milestones: Honor the minor triumphs! Recognizing your accomplishments, whether they're jogging an extra mile, finishing a week of exercise, or just feeling more energized, motivates you to keep going and reinforces positive behavior.

Making Use of Activity Challenges and Reminders

It's time to maintain your course now that you have established and modified your goals. There are features on the Garmin Forerunner that are intended to hold you accountable.

1. Activity Reminders: Take advantage of this function. Seniors, who may forget to get up and move after spending a lot of time sitting down, may especially benefit from this. Set a reminder to stretch lightly or go for a quick stroll every hour. It's a mild prod that can have a big impact on your general wellness.

2. Join Challenges: participate in challenges with friends or through the Garmin Connect community if you enjoy a competitive atmosphere. These could be virtual races, step challenges, or even challenges that are based on how much time is spent working out. Your fitness journey becomes a shared experience rather than just a personal objective when you interact with others.

3. Establish a Connection: The Garmin community is large and encouraging. Giving others access to your objectives and advancements can inspire you and hold you accountable. On their path, you might even motivate someone else! Join forums or social media communities devoted to Garmin users to exchange advice and recognize accomplishments.

Establishing and personalizing your exercise objectives is a liberating process that establishes the foundation for your health path. By utilizing the features offered by the Garmin Forerunner 165 and 965, you're creating a lifestyle that aligns with your goals rather than merely monitoring your progress. These actions will assist you in developing a rewarding and long-lasting exercise experience, regardless of whether you're an avid fitness enthusiast pushing yourself to the maximum or an elderly person concentrating on your health. You can achieve your goals; now is the time to enjoy the trip that lies ahead!

Chapter 3
Examining the potential of GPS navigation
How to Utilize GPS for Activities in the Outdoors

You can take your outdoor experiences to the next level by utilizing the GPS capabilities of your Garmin Forerunner 165 or 965. Imagine choosing a running route that not only measures your distance but also improves your experience, or embarking on a trip without the fear of getting lost. GPS functionality is your reliable partner, providing unparalleled accuracy when you run, cycle, or hike.

An overview of GPS features for different purposes

What comes to mind when you think about GPS? It may be your car's voice guiding you through congested roadways. However, GPS is capable of much more in the fitness space. This technology allows fitness aficionados to precisely track their distance, pace, and route, which helps them get the most out of their workouts. It provides seniors with a safety net by providing position monitoring and real-time navigation, which makes outdoor activities stress-free and pleasurable.

Let's see how GPS functions for different outdoor pursuits:

1. Running: The Garmin Forerunner tracks your route, pace, and distance traveled using GPS once you put on your shoes and hit the road. Anyone trying to get better at running or get ready for a race needs to know this information. With the watch's immediate feedback, you can modify your pace and endurance as you go.

2. Cycling: It's thrilling to ride a bike through narrow streets or twisting paths, but getting lost might ruin your trip. You can comfortably explore new routes with GPS. To make sure you stay on the intended course, the Forerunner will track your bicycle route and even provide turn-by-turn guidance. Additionally, it records your speed so you can see how you're doing over time.

3. Hiking: Although nature is your playground, it can be difficult to navigate uncharted territory. Your forerunner's GPS function serves as your guide, giving you crucial details regarding elevation, distance, and the anticipated time to reach your objective. Seniors who like to explore the great outdoors without worrying about getting lost will find it extremely helpful.

Procedures for Using the Garmin Connect App to Create and Save Routes

It is simple to create and save routes using the Garmin Connect app. This function not only makes workout planning easier, but it also makes outdoor activities more exciting. To get started, take these easy steps:

1. Launch the Garmin Connect App: Select the "Activities" area after synchronizing your Garmin Forerunner with the app. A list of your prior workouts can be found here, but for the time being, we'll concentrate on coming up with a new path.

2. Choose 'Create a Course': Inside the application, tap the 'More' option (the three dots) in the lower right corner. Select the option labeled "Courses." The magic happens right here!

3. Pick Your Activity Type: Decide the activity type you are designing the route for. Depending on your preference, the app will customize the suggested courses for jogging, cycling, or hiking.

4. Map Out Your path: Plot your path using the interactive map. To get points along the way, just tap the map. By selecting picturesque routes, staying off of congested roads, or adding particular places you'd like to see, you may personalize your itinerary.

5. Save Your Route: After you're pleased with your itinerary, name it anything that describes your journey, like "Mountain Trail Adventure" or "Scenic Park Loop."

Click "Save," and presto! Your Garmin gadget is prepared to sync your journey.

6. Sync to Your Garmin Forerunner: Make sure the app is linked to your device. Your updated route will be synced to your watch when you tap "Sync."

7. Begin Your Adventure: Choose your forerunner's route when you're prepared to start your outdoor activity. You can easily follow your intended course with the watch's real-time input, which includes distance and pace.

You're improving your experience overall by being proficient with GPS technology, not just tracking your moves. GPS turns outdoor activities into life-changing experiences, whether you're running to break personal records, cycling to new heights, or hiking to discover the natural world. Accept technology and use your Garmin Forerunner to help you reach and surpass your fitness objectives. Awaiting you is your next adventure!

Getting Around with Your Precursor

Consider this scenario: you're running, the sun is lowering, and you've just stepped onto a trail you've never been on before. Although the excitement of adventure is thrilling, a glimmer of doubt soon appears. Suppose you become lost. This is where your Garmin Forerunner 165 or 965 excels, turning what might otherwise be a tense situation into a smooth voyage through the splendor of nature. Whether you're a senior looking to protect yourself or a fitness fanatic looking for new routes, using your Forerunner to navigate is about more than simply finding your way—it's about improving your outdoor experiences.

Guidelines for Using the Navigation Features While Engaging in Activities

Using your watch to navigate is as simple as a few taps. First, make sure the GPS signal is strong and your smartphone is charged. Here's a useful, step-by-step manual to get you started:

1. Choose Your Activity: To view the activity menu, press the button. Select from choices such as "Run," "Bike," or "Hike." Every choice makes sure you obtain the most accurate data by optimizing the parameters for that particular activity.

2. Go to Navigation Settings: After choosing your activity, go to the menu and choose "Navigation." Here, you have the option of making a new route or following one that has already been stored. Choosing a pre-planned route is a smart option if you're traveling to a new place.

3. Creating a Route: Use the Garmin Connect software on your smartphone to create your own route. Plotting your route according to distance, difficulty, and even picturesque views is possible. To prepare for your upcoming excursion, sync this route with your watch.

4. Begin Your Journey: Just click "Start" once you've chosen or created a route. Your progress will be tracked by your watch, which will show your distance traveled, pace, and anticipated arrival time at your destination.

5. Comply with the Navigation Prompts: Your Forerunner will ensure you stay on course by providing you with clear on-screen guidance and vibrations at strategic points as you progress. Your path is shown on the screen, and the watch will recalculate and direct you back on course if you get off course.

Using your Forerunner to navigate improves your workout in addition to helping you find your route. A fitness enthusiast might, for example, choose a new running route and measure their progress while relishing the excitement of discovery. A senior user, on the other hand, can go out with confidence because they have a trustworthy guide.

Comprehending Live Tracking and Alerts for Safety

Particularly when going outdoors, safety is crucial. There are features on the Garmin Forerunner that are intended to keep you safe while you're moving.

1. Configuring Live Tracking: Before leaving, think about turning on the Garmin Connect app's LiveTrack feature. This enables real-time location tracking for friends and relatives. It's an excellent safety net, particularly for elderly people who would prefer outdoor activities to be done alone. Your loved ones will know where to look for you in case something goes wrong.

2. Safety notifications: The Forerunner has customized notifications that let you know when something important changes. For example, the watch vibrates to alert you if your heart rate rises above a predetermined threshold. To make sure you stay aware of your surroundings without taking your eyes off the road, you may also set alerts for approaching curves or distance milestones.

3. Making Use of the Incident Detection Function: This function can be quite helpful for people who are participating in physically demanding activities. The watch has the ability to notify your emergency contacts of your location in the event of a fall or abrupt stop. It's a feature made to let you enjoy the freedom to engage in your favorite hobbies with peace of mind.

4. Getting Around in Urban Environments: The Forerunner's GPS can help you stay on course even while you're moving through congested neighborhoods or city streets. It improves your experience by warning you of impending intersections and even pointing you in the direction of the closest landmarks or facilities, such as restrooms or drinking fountains.

Knowing how to use your Forerunner gives you the confidence to explore the world, whether you're going for a strenuous run, a relaxing stroll, or an exciting trek. Each trip becomes a carefully thought-out adventure thanks to the mix of dependable navigation tools and safety alarms, which frees you from worrying about getting lost and lets you enjoy the excitement of movement. Enjoy the freedom that comes with knowing that your Garmin Forerunner will keep you safe, healthy, and able to explore new routes.

Chapter 4
SolvingTypical Problems

Recognizing typical issues

To guarantee a seamless and pleasurable experience with your fitness watch, the first step is to identify frequent issues with your Garmin Forerunner 165 and 965. You rely on your gadget to function consistently, whether you're a senior trying to keep an eye on your health or a fitness enthusiast. But like any technology, problems can arise from time to time. Let's examine some common problems consumers have and the telltale symptoms of a gadget breakdown.

Issues with Syncing

Syncing troubles between the Garmin Connect app and the Garmin Forerunner are among the most frequent problems users encounter. Your workout data may not sync or the app may not recognize your device.

Indications of Synching Problems:

• **Data Not Appearing:** Your data does not appear in the app following a workout. This can indicate that the activity was not properly saved by the watch.

• **App Notification Errors:** This is a serious concern if the app keeps telling you that it is unable to connect or sync.

• **Bluetooth Connection Issues:** Syncing will be impacted if your watch keeps disconnecting from your phone or does not pair when you attempt to pair it.

Realistic Remedies:

• **Verify Bluetooth Settings:** Make sure your watch is within range and that Bluetooth is turned on on your smartphone.

• **Restart Both Devices:** In many cases, connectivity problems can be fixed by just restarting your smartphone and watch.

• **Update Software:** Make sure the Garmin Connect app and your watch are both up to date. These updates frequently enhance speed and address issues.

A Battery's Life

Battery life is another issue that many Garmin users have. Battery life can vary depending on features, settings, and usage patterns, and nobody wants to be mid-workout with a dead gadget.

Indications of Battery Problems:

• **Rapid Drain:** An issue is obviously present if you observe that the battery percentage reduces noticeably in a short period of time.

• **Inconsistent Charging:** You should look into why your watch doesn't charge even when it is plugged in.

• Overheating: An underlying problem may be indicated if your device feels abnormally hot while charging.

Realistic Remedies:

• **Optimize Settings:** When a feature isn't required, turn it off, such as GPS or heart rate tracking. Battery life can also be preserved by reducing the brightness.

• **Frequent Charging:** To preserve the best possible battery health, try charging your watch on a regular basis rather than waiting for the battery to run entirely flat.

• **Examine the charging wire:** Inconsistent charging may result from a damaged or worn-out charging cable. Replace the cable if it seems ragged or doesn't fit tightly.

Symptoms and indicators of device failure

You can avoid more serious problems later on by spotting a Garmin watch issue early. It's critical to recognize the warning indicators that anything is amiss.

Common signs and symptoms:

• **Unresponsive Touchscreen:** You may need to troubleshoot your watch if the touchscreen is not reacting to swipes or touches.

• **Random Restarts:** If your device restarts itself or shuts down without warning, there may be a more serious problem.

• **Messages about errors:** note any errors that appear on the screen. They can offer important details on what's broken.

Methodical Procedures for Diagnosis:

• **Soft Reset:** Hold down the power button until your device restarts to try a soft reset if it stops responding. This usually fixes little bugs.

• **Check for upgrades:** Make sure the most recent software version is installed on your watch because upgrades might fix known problems and enhance functionality.

• **Contact assistance:** Please do not hesitate to contact Garmin assistance if the issue continues. If necessary, they can suggest repair choices or walk you through more troubleshooting procedures.

As a user, you can maintain optimal performance on your Garmin Forerunner 165 or 965 by being aware of these typical issues and their symptoms. Whether you're trying to maintain a healthy lifestyle or set new personal records, you can make sure that your fitness journey stays uninterrupted and focused on your objectives if you have the necessary information and resources at your disposal.

Efficient Solutions for Troubleshooting

It can be like navigating a maze in the realm of technology. When your Garmin Forerunner 165 or 965 doesn't work as you expect it to, you may find yourself at a standstill and a little agitated. Don't worry, though! Good troubleshooting techniques can come in handy, and by following a few simple steps, you can resolve the majority of frequent problems and get your fitness watch operating normally again.

Methodical fixes for typical issues

1. Problems with Syncing

It can be annoying, particularly after a strenuous workout, if your Forerunner isn't synchronizing with the Garmin Connect app. To get things back on track, follow these steps:

• **Verify Bluetooth is Enabled:** Verify that Bluetooth is turned on on both your smartphone and smartwatch. This straightforward step is frequently disregarded.

• **Restart Both Devices:** Occasionally, a fast reboot is sufficient. Switch off and then switch back on your phone and Forerunner.

• **To reconnect,** use the Garmin Connect app, navigate to the settings, and choose your device. To restart the connection, disconnect it and reconnect your watch.

2. Too-fast battery drain

A watch that can't keep up with your lifestyle is the most aggravating thing ever! Try these suggestions if you observe that your battery is draining more quickly than you anticipated:

• **Modify Display Settings:** Cut down on screen timeout length and brightness. Your display uses more power the brighter it is.

• **Turn Off Unused Features:** To conserve battery life, turn off GPS, alerts, and heart rate tracking when not in use.

• **Update Firmware Frequently:** Garmin regularly publishes firmware updates that might increase battery life. Check the Garmin Connect app for updates.

3. The GPS is not connecting

GPS is essential for tracking your path, whether you're going for a run or a walk. Try these methods if your watch is having trouble picking up a signal:

- **Step outside:** Indoor GPS signals can be weak. Go outside where you can see the sky clearly.

- **Empty the cache:** Sometimes a refresh of the GPS settings is necessary. To remove any outdated data, go into settings and reset the GPS.

- **Verify Firmware Update:** Updates frequently improve GPS performance, so look for the most recent firmware in the Garmin Connect app.

4. Erroneous heart rate measurements

For any workout fanatic, getting precise heart rate readings is crucial. Take into consideration the following actions if your forerunner is showing odd numbers:

- **Verify the Watch's Fit:** Make sure your watch fits comfortably around your wrist. Inaccurate readings can result from a loose fit.

- **Wipe the Sensors:** Sweat and debris can clog the heart rate monitor. Use a gentle, dry cloth to wipe the back of your watch.

- **Turn Activity Tracking On or Off:** Turning the heart rate monitor on and off can occasionally cause the sensors to re-calibrate.

Advice on Preserving the Longevity and Performance of Devices

Maintaining your Garmin Forerunner prolongs its life in addition to enhancing performance. Here are some useful pointers:

- **Frequent Updates:** Make sure your gadget is up to date. To guarantee you have the newest features and bug fixes, use the Garmin Connect app to periodically check for software updates.

- **Care for Storage:** When not in use, keep your watch somewhere dry and cold. Keep it away from moisture and extremely high or low temperatures, as these can harm its internal parts.

- **Routine Cleaning:** To avoid perspiration, dust, and grime accumulation, particularly around the sensors, clean your watch on a regular basis. A basic cloth made of microfiber can work miracles.

• **Battery Health:** Charge your watch to roughly 50% before putting it away if you won't be using it for a long time. This procedure keeps batteries healthy.

• **Seek care:** If you run into problems that go beyond simple troubleshooting, don't be afraid to contact Garmin customer care. Their staff is prepared to help you.

Your experience with the Garmin Forerunner 165 and 965 can be greatly improved by incorporating these maintenance suggestions and troubleshooting techniques into your daily routine. Your device will function at its best and go with you on many future fitness trips if you take a little preventative care of it!

Chapter 5
Using Hints and Techniques to Improve Your Experience

Changing the Face and Settings of Your Watch

Your Garmin Forerunner 165 & 965 is a customized companion on your health journey, not just a fitness tracker. Changing the settings and face of your watch is one of the most enjoyable ways to show off your own style and improve your experience. Making the watch operate for you, giving you the information you desire, and showcasing your individual style are more important than merely looking good.

Guidelines for Modifying the Faces and Layouts of watches

Go to your smartphone's Garmin Connect app to start personalizing your watch face. After pairing the app with your watch, take these actions:

1. Launch the Garmin Connect application: To open the app, tap on it. Make sure your watch is Bluetooth-enabled.

2. Click the "Device" icon, which is located in the menu: Your Forerunner 165 or 965 will be visible when you navigate to your connected devices.

3. Select "Watch Faces" to view the selection of watch faces that are compatible with your device. Everything from vibrant, data-rich displays to minimalist designs are available.

4. Pick Your Preferred Watch Face: Navigate through the selections. You can preview items by tapping on them if you like them. Frequently, you will be able to alter specific components, such as the colors and the data that is shown.

5. Sync the Changes: After choosing your watch face, make sure it matches your device and allow the app to sync it. Your watch will have a completely different appearance in a matter of seconds!

6. Real-world illustration: Let's say you enjoy running outside and are a fitness enthusiast. While a senior user might choose a straightforward design that plainly indicates the time and step count, you could prefer a watch face that boldly displays your current heart rate and pace. This personalization makes your important information easy to find.

Changing configurations for the best results

Changing settings improves your Garmin Forerunner's usability and functionality in addition to its appearance. Here are some useful settings tweaks to maximize the functionality of your watch:

1. Brightness Settings: You want your watch's display to be readable in direct sunlight. On the other hand, a high brightness level at night can be glaring. To change the brightness:

Press and hold your watch's Light button.

Locate the Settings icon on the touch screen, then select Display.

Change the backlight's brightness to suit your tastes. When not in use, you can also configure the backlight timeout to save battery life.

2. Handling Notifications: It's important to stay in touch, but receiving too many alerts can be stressful. Choose which alerts you want to receive:

Launch the Garmin Connect application.

Select Smart Notifications under Settings. Call, text, email, and app alert notifications can all be turned on or off here.

Configure it so that you only get the most crucial updates, free from interruptions.

3. Customizing Activity Notifications: Activity notifications might help you stay motivated if you're working toward a particular fitness objective.

Open the Garmin Connect app and navigate to Activity Settings.

Select the parameters you wish to get alerts for, such as pace, heart rate, or distance, and establish thresholds that will cause them to sound.

Imagine your Forerunner buzzing softly as you cross each mile of a half marathon. This tailored support might make all the difference in helping you achieve your objectives.

Making Use of Advanced Features

The Garmin Forerunner 165 & 965 is more than just a fitness tracker; it's a weather forecaster, music player, and personal coach all in one! Let's explore the cutting-edge features that can improve your fitness journey and simplify your life.

Examining Music Control

Imagine this: Your favorite music drops the ideal beat while you're halfway through a run, your feet thudding on the pavement. You can manage your music right from your watch when you use the Garmin Forerunner. Syncing your playlist is simple, regardless of whether you're an Apple Music enthusiast or a Spotify user.

Go to your smartphone's Garmin Connect app to configure music control. Choose your favorite music provider under the "Music" settings, then connect your account. Playlists can be downloaded straight to your watch once you're connected. This means you can move freely without your phone. You know the power of motivation as a fitness enthusiast. You can get through the hardest miles with the help of music. Make a playlist that appeals to your soul, whether it's upbeat pop songs or soothing classical music for your downtime. Adding a little rhythm to your workout might make a big difference.

Keeping abreast of weather notifications

The weather can be erratic, particularly if you're devoted to being outside. With real-time weather alerts on your wrist, the Garmin Forerunner can keep you informed. The days of unexpectedly getting caught in a strong wind or running in a sudden shower are long gone. Make sure the Garmin Connect app is linked to your watch in order to enable weather updates. Go to the settings after syncing, then grant location access. Throughout the day, the watch will notify you of any changes and pull local weather forecasts. Before starting your morning jog or afternoon bike trip, you can check the temperature or radar on your watch.

These features can be quite helpful to seniors who are interested in health monitoring. Being aware of the weather might help you steer clear of extremes that could harm your health. A low-impact indoor workout could be a better option if it's a hot day.

Leveraging Virtual Coaching's Power

Utilize the Garmin Forerunner's virtual coaching capabilities if you want to step up your fitness game. For people who thrive on accountability but might not have access to a personal trainer, this feature is quite helpful.

The watch provides guided exercises that may be modified to meet your objectives and degree of fitness.

Go to your watch's "Training" menu to make use of this feature. You can choose from a variety of routines here, including yoga, weight training, and interval training. You can concentrate on your form instead of looking at a timer or a complex chart thanks to the watch's auditory cues and on-screen instructions.

Seniors can learn safe and efficient exercises that are suited to their abilities with the help of virtual coaching. Without the intimidating atmosphere of a gym, it's a fantastic way to add variation to your program.

Suggestions for integrations and third-party apps

Numerous third-party apps are available inside the Garmin ecosystem to improve your experience even more. One such example is MyFitnessPal, which tracks your diet in tandem with your workouts by effortlessly integrating with your Garmin gadget. This all-encompassing method can assist you in comprehending how your dietary decisions affect your recuperation and effectiveness.

Strava is another notable app that is popular with both cyclists and runners. You may join challenges, compare your efforts with others, and even find new routes with Strava's community features. In addition to improving data recording, connecting your Garmin gadget to Strava keeps you motivated through healthy competition.

Finally, think about including Headspace or Calm for guided meditations if you're investigating mindfulness and mental wellness. Stress management is important for everyone, but it's especially important for seniors who are concerned about their health. Improving general well-being can result from taking some time to relax and regroup.

Changing Your Fitness Path

By making use of these sophisticated capabilities, you can turn your fitness journey into an interesting, multifaceted experience rather than only recording steps or heart rates. Imagine this: The weather is ideal, you're motivated by your favorite music, your virtual coach leads you through intervals, and you go for a run. Every workout feels new and energizing, and the entire world turns into your gym.

The Garmin Forerunner 165 and 965 give you the ability to take charge of your health and fitness, regardless of your level of dedication to fitness or your age and desire to lead an active lifestyle. Accept these cutting-edge features and see how they can improve your general quality of life as well as your exercises.

Chapter 6
Genuine User Narratives and Community Assistance
Motivating Technological Transformations

The realm of fitness tracking is about actual people changing their lives, not just about metrics and stats. The Garmin Forerunner 165 and 965 have grown to be indispensable partners for many people on their paths to wellness and health. Let's examine some motivational tales that demonstrate how technology may bring about amazing changes when paired with willpower.

Consider the case of 42-year-old Sarah, a mother of three. For years, she had battled her weight, frequently feeling overburdened by the responsibilities of family life. She came across a post from a friend who had just begun using the Garmin Forerunner 965 one day while perusing social media. She made the decision to purchase one for herself after being intrigued by its GPS capabilities and fitness tracking functions.

During family walks, Sarah started using her new watch to monitor her heart rate and steps. What began as a casual neighborhood walk swiftly developed into regular running sessions. With the aid of her Garmin, she was able to track her progress, set pace alerts, and even listen to her favorite music while she ran her first 5K. She felt stronger and more confident every week, both as a mother and as a runner. After all, Sarah says that her first 5K experience was "life-changing" as she crossed the finish line. Her entire perspective on life, not just her exercise regimen, had changed as a result of the Garmin.

Next up is Tom, a 68-year-old retiree who has always taken immense satisfaction in maintaining an active lifestyle. But he was sidelined and concerned about his health after suffering a knee ailment. When Tom first heard about the Garmin Forerunner 165 from a buddy, he was apprehensive. Technology had never been his thing. But he was impressed by the device's ease of use.

Tom set a modest goal of 5,000 steps per day and started using the watch to count his daily steps. He added walking intervals to his regimen and progressively raised his target when his strength returned. He was reassured by the heart rate monitoring feature during workouts, and the watch's reminders nudged him to move when he had been still for too long. Tom was able to learn from others and share his success when he joined a local walking group that also used Garmin devices.

Tom finally switched to light jogging and is currently preparing for a charity walk after being motivated by the companionship and the information his watch offered. He beams with delight as he says, "The Garmin opened up a whole new social world; it didn't just help me get back on my feet."

These anecdotes highlight the significant effects of wearing a Garmin fitness watch, but the real magic is found in the communities that have grown up around these gadgets. Through local meetups, social media groups, and online forums, many users interact and exchange advice, difficulties, and support. This feeling of inclusion can be very inspiring.

Sharing accomplishments, such as finishing a run of workouts or setting a new personal record, fosters accountability and a network of support for fitness aficionados. This community component helps seniors feel connected and encouraged, which lessens the loneliness of the journey. By exchanging Garmin screenshots and congratulating one another on their accomplishments, people transform what may have been a solo pursuit into a group health adventure.

Think about the influence of Garmin user-focused social media groups. Numerous Facebook groups exist where participants share their fitness accomplishments, participate in challenges, and give and receive advice. Imagine posting updates about your progress on a community website and getting comments and likes from those who are following your path. It inspires you and strengthens your sense of belonging to a greater whole.

To sum up, the experiences of Sarah, Tom, and innumerable others serve as a reminder that everyone's path to health is different. More than just fitness trackers, the Garmin Forerunner 165 and 965 offer doors to motivation, camaraderie, and personal development. Regardless of your level of experience, keep in mind that every little step matters and that community support may help you reach new heights on your path. Accept technology, tell your story, and use it to inspire others and yourself to change.

Creating a Community of Support

It might be intimidating to navigate the huge world of technology and fitness alone. That's where communal power comes into play. You're not simply embracing a fitness tool when you join the Garmin Forerunner community; you're joining a thriving community of enthusiasts who share your objectives, struggles, and successes.

The Value of Using Social Media and Forums to Engage Communities

Imagine the satisfaction of resolving a single, recurring syncing issue with someone who has been in your position or the excitement of sharing your first 5K run that was flawlessly monitored by your Garmin watch. Because it puts you in touch with people who can provide support, guidance, and companionship, community engagement is crucial. It improves your path to improved health and turns solo workouts into group activities.

Social media groups and online forums devoted to Garmin devices are informational gold mines. Users can celebrate successes, exchange advice, and post queries on these networks. These exchanges can result in new exercise partners, practical tips for maximizing your Garmin settings, or even simply a little friendly rivalry to keep you going if you're a fitness enthusiast. It's never too late to start a fitness adventure, since the community can provide elders with inspiration, motivation, and technical help.

Think about participating in forums like the Garmin Community, where people talk about everything from troubleshooting to exercise regimens. These conversations can generate concepts, motivate fresh problems, and offer answers you might not have thought of. A lot of individuals post their own success stories, which can be really inspiring. A fitness enthusiast may find new techniques to improve their training routine, while a senior may read about someone their age finishing a marathon.

Advice for Getting in Touch with Other Garmin Users and Exchanging Stories

1. Get involved: Don't just observe; take part! Ask questions, reply to others, and share your experiences. Someone else might benefit greatly from your insights.

2. Make Use of Social Media: Facebook, Instagram, and Twitter are excellent places to meet other Garmin users. Utilize hashtags such as #GarminCommunity or #GarminForerunner to interact with other users and locate posts. You can build relationships and start conversations by asking for advice or posting pictures of your workouts.

3. Join local groups: Garmin devices are used by many cities' cycling or running groups. In addition to offering encouragement, joining a local organization connects you with like-minded individuals.

4. Take Part in Challenges: A lot of communities hold events that can promote involvement and a spirit of friendly competitiveness, such as step counts or distance races. Working together to finish a task can foster accountability and companionship.

5. Share Your Progress: Sharing your accomplishments can motivate others and strengthen your relationships, whether it's a new personal best, a trek you've finished, or just your daily steps. Honor accomplishments, no matter how minor, as they add to the greater story of community support.

6. Attend Garmin Events: Seek out regional or online Garmin gatherings. These get-togethers can offer priceless in-person relationships and user insights. They frequently feature knowledgeable speakers who may impart their expertise and offer advice on making the most of your gadget.

7. Offer Assistance: Don't be afraid to share your knowledge or expertise, whether it be an exercise regimen, dietary guidance, or troubleshooting techniques. Providing assistance can be as fulfilling as getting it.

Participating actively in these groups will improve your individual Garmin Forerunner experience while also fostering a positive network where everyone benefits from one another's success. A more satisfying fitness journey might result from the friendships made, the tales exchanged, and the support offered.

The encouraging community around the Garmin Forerunner serves as a reminder that we are not alone in our fitness endeavors in a world where loneliness can be prevalent. These relationships may give you the inspiration, information, and support you need to keep going forward, whether you're a senior keeping an eye on your health or a fitness enthusiast aiming for your next objective. As you set out on this thrilling journey, embrace the community, share your experiences, and allow others to motivate you.